HALLOWEEN
OCT. 31
WELCOME TO ZOMBIE PARTY!
ENJOY

Happy Halloween
Zombie
Party
Coloring Book
Sandy Mahony & Mary Lou Brown

ZOMBIE INFECTION
R.I.P.
RIP
RIP
R.I.P.
RIP
RIP
RIP
Zombie
OUTBREAK

Where's the party?

It's on a dead end street!

I need a job!

We're hiring!

I love a woman with BRAAAINS!

HELP!

I'm dying to have you for dinner!

Where's the monSTORE?

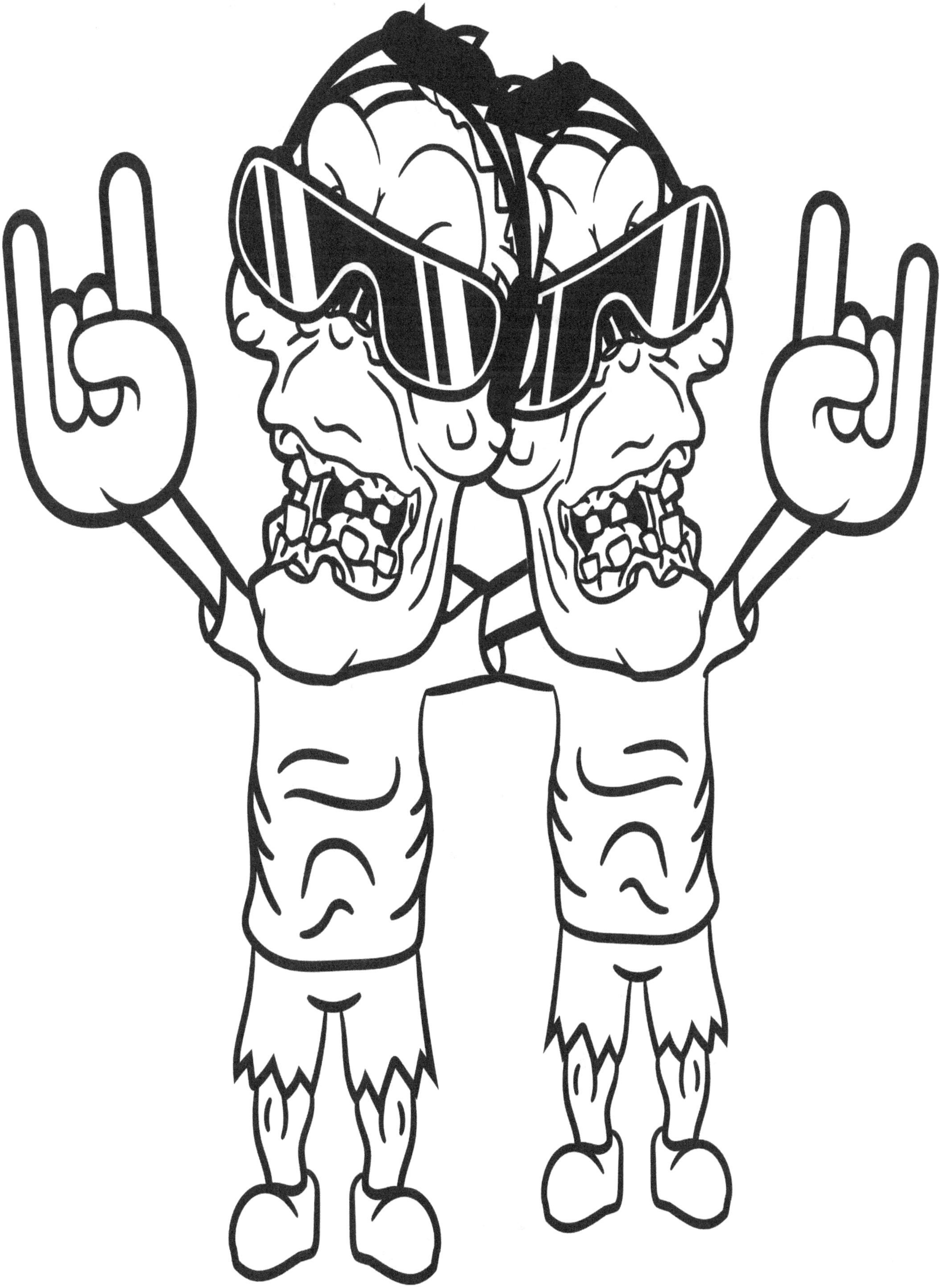

Enjoy the Apocalypse!

It's been a great life!

He lost his mind!

Where have you been all my life?

RIP
Where are the girls?

adventurelearningpress.com

www.ingramcontent.com/pod-product-compliance
Lightning Source LLC
Chambersburg PA
CBHW081805280526
45789CB00008B/3004
* 9 7 8 1 5 3 7 7 4 3 2 6 4 *